Eclipses

by Grace Hansen

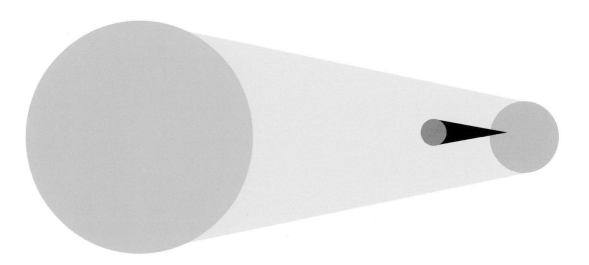

Abdo Kids Jumbo is an Imprint of Abdo Kids
abdobooks.com

abdobooks.com

Published by Abdo Kids, a division of ABDO, P.O. Box 398166, Minneapolis, Minnesota 55439.
Copyright © 2020 by Abdo Consulting Group, Inc. International copyrights reserved in all countries.
No part of this book may be reproduced in any form without written permission from the publisher.
Abdo Kids Jumbo™ is a trademark and logo of Abdo Kids.

Printed in the United States of America, North Mankato, Minnesota.

102019

012020

Photo Credits: iStock, NASA, Shutterstock

Production Contributors: Teddy Borth, Jennie Forsberg, Grace Hansen
Design Contributors: Dorothy Toth, Pakou Moua

Library of Congress Control Number: 2019941210
Publisher's Cataloging-in-Publication Data

Names: Hansen, Grace, author.

Title: Eclipses / by Grace Hansen

Description: Minneapolis, Minnesota : Abdo Kids, 2020 | Series: Sky lights | Includes online resources
    and index.

Identifiers: ISBN 9781532189074 (lib. bdg.) | ISBN 9781532189562 (ebook) | ISBN 9781098200541
    (Read-to-Me ebook)

Subjects: LCSH: Lunar eclipses--Juvenile literature. | Solar eclipses--Juvenile literature. |
    Light--Juvenile literature. | Astronomy--Juvenile literature. | Eclipses--Juvenile literature. | Space--
    Juvenile literature. | Sun--Juvenile literature. | Moon--Juvenile literature.

Classification: DDC 523--dc23

Table of Contents

What Is an Eclipse?

An eclipse is when one space object moves into the shadow of another.

5

An eclipse can happen to any space object. But it is easiest for us to see eclipses of the sun and moon.

The earth **orbits** the sun.

The moon orbits the earth.

An eclipse can happen when

all of these bodies are in line.

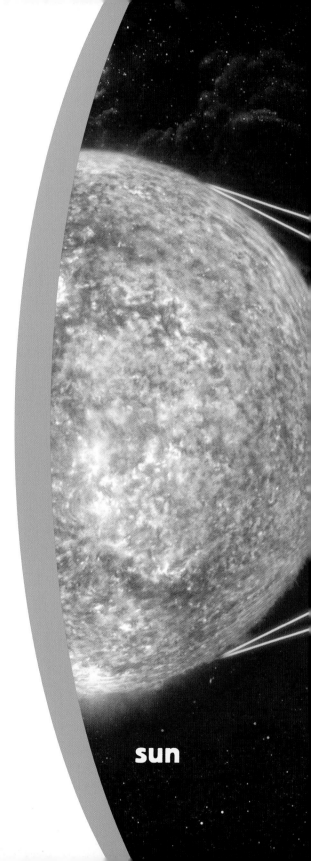

sun

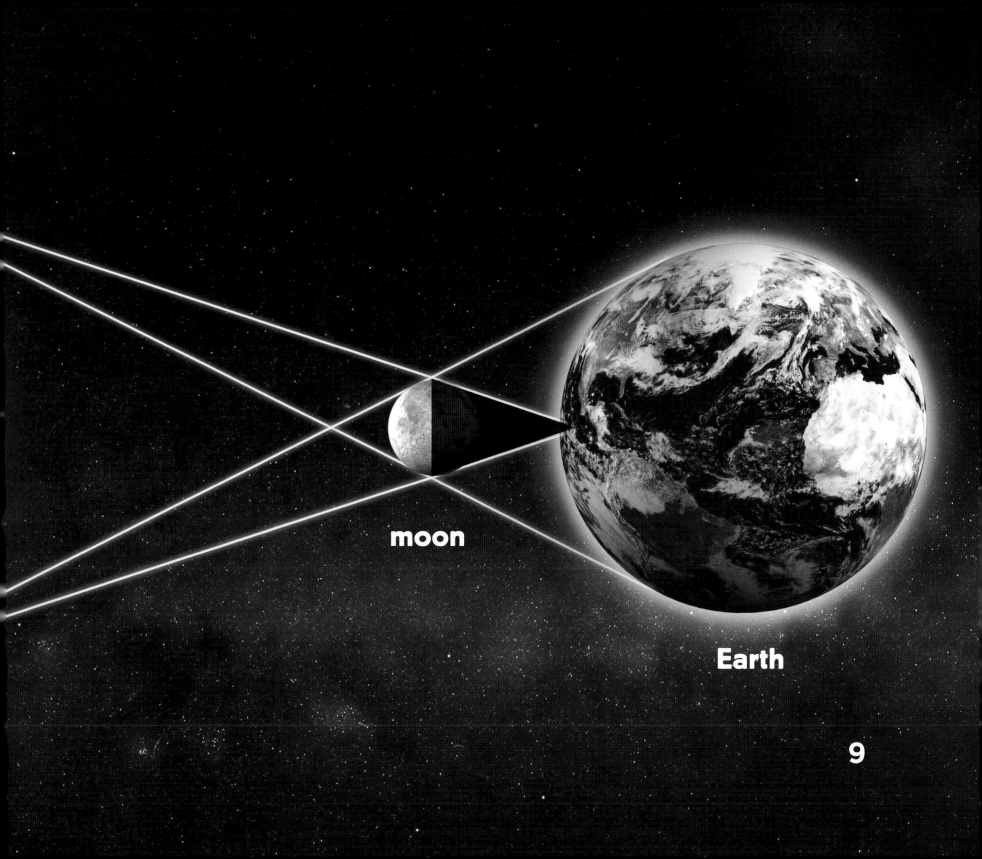

moon

Earth

Solar Eclipse

In a solar eclipse, the moon moves between the sun and Earth. A shadow is cast on Earth. The sky gets darker.

A total solar eclipse is not
very rare, but seeing one is.
This is because where you
are on Earth matters.

13

The earth spins as it **orbits** the sun. Earth's position in an eclipse changes what people see. And people live on many points of Earth's surface.

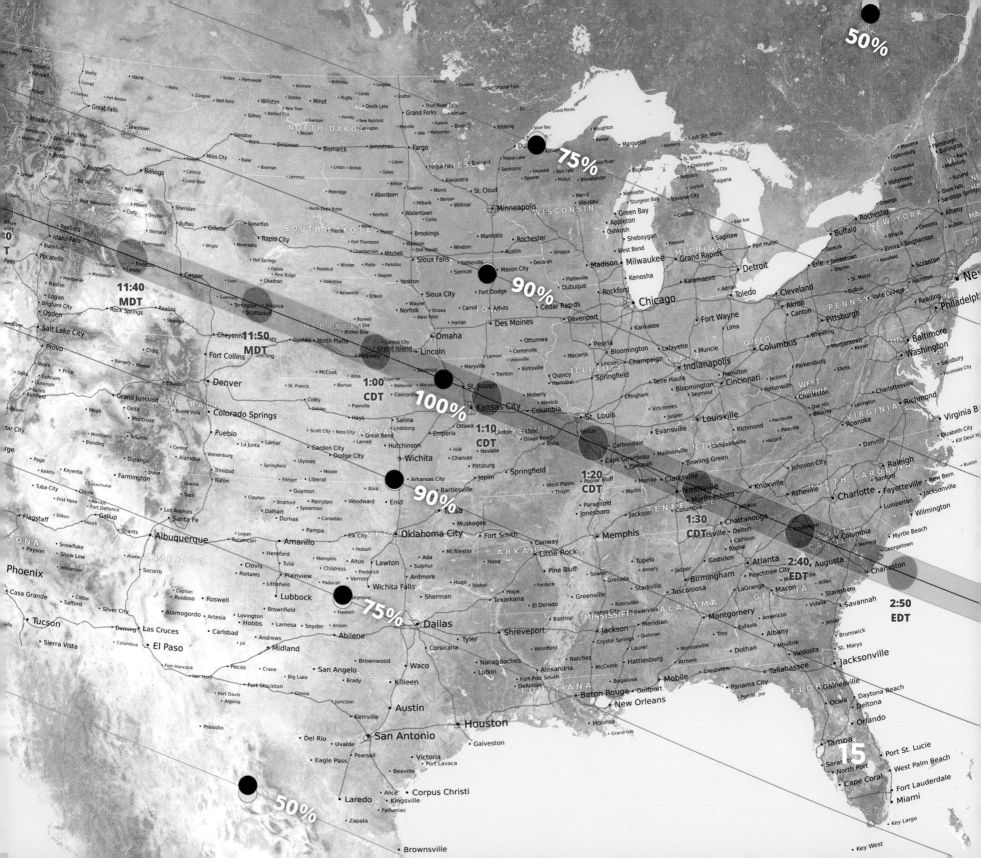

Watching a solar eclipse is an exciting experience. But looking at one without eye protection is dangerous. Wearing safe viewing glasses is important!

Lunar Eclipse

A lunar eclipse happens when the earth is between the sun and moon. The moon moves into Earth's shadow. This blocks the sun's light from **reflecting** off of the moon.

sun

Earth

moon

Lunar eclipses happen less than solar eclipses. A lunar eclipse can only happen during a **full moon**. But when it happens, it is visible to more than half of Earth!

More Facts

- Eclipses happen in all galaxies. Not just our own.

- The last total solar eclipse seen in Los Angeles, California, was in 1724. The next one there is scheduled for the year 3290. That's 1,566 years between totalities!

- The temperature on Earth drops when there is a solar eclipse. This is because the sun's light heats the earth.

Glossary

cast – to give off or project.

full moon – the moon when it is on the side of Earth that is opposite the sun and looks, from Earth, like a complete circle.

orbit – a curved path in which a planet or other space body moves in a circle around another body.

reflect – a body throwing back light without absorbing it.

23

Index

Abdo Kids ONLINE
FREE! ONLINE MULTIMEDIA RESOURCES

Visit abdokids.com to access crafts, games, videos, and more!

Use Abdo Kids code
SEK9074
or scan this QR code!